W9-CLA-813

Zoom in on
RESPECT FOR
AUTHORITY

Rita Santos

Enslow Publishing
101 W. 23rd Street
Suite 240
New York, NY 10011
USA

enslow.com

WORDS TO KNOW

authority The power to influence the thoughts or behavior of others.

citizen A member of a community.

civic Having to do with the community.

enforce To carry out.

evacuate To leave an area to avoid danger.

meteorologist Someone who studies the atmosphere and weather.

moral Good and right.

oath A formal promise.

obligation A responsibility someone is required to perform.

specialized Having to do with one certain area.

transparency Being open and honest about actions.

CONTENTS

People in authority are responsible for helping the community.

What Is Authority?

People with authority have been given control over certain places or situations. Usually people gain authority through years of education and specialized training. They have the power to make decisions, give orders, and enforce rules. People with authority have a responsibility to always do what is best for the community. Authority figures earn the trust of their communities by keeping the promises they make.

Our Civic Duties

Respecting authority is one of our civic duties—our responsibilities as community members. It is also considered a civic virtue. What is a civic virtue? Civic refers to our community. A virtue is an idea or behavior that is considered good and moral. So a civic virtue is something we do or believe that is for the good of the whole community. Respecting authority means following the advice and directions of people in positions of power. This is good for everyone in the community.

Fast Fact

Doctors take an oath to "do no harm."

Authority in Different Places

Your teacher is an authority in your classroom. Teachers are authority figures because they have the knowledge needed to help students learn and grow. Police officers have been

Your parents use their authority to teach you and keep you safe.

trained and given the authority to protect and serve their communities. If a police officer asks you to do something, she is probably trying to keep you safe. But remember: police officers have to follow the rules, too. This means that if an officer wants to ask you questions, your parent or guardian needs to be with you. You should not be afraid to remind authority figures of the rules.

Why Should We Respect Authority?

There is more information in the world than any one person could ever learn. People gain authority in subjects by spending years learning about them. They have earned their authority through hard work and education.

Achieving Goals

Good citizens want everyone in their communities to be smart, healthy, and safe. Respecting authority helps us achieve

Listening to your teachers shows that you respect their authority.

these goals. You may not want to stop talking when your teacher tells you to, but you must listen in order to learn. Being quiet during your lessons helps your classmates pay attention as well, because they are not distracted. Respecting your teacher's authority is good for your whole class.

Questioning Authority

No one is right all the time. Sometimes people with authority make mistakes. If a person with authority tells you to do something you know is wrong or that will hurt someone else, you don't have to do it. Asking authority figures questions isn't rude if it is done in a respectful way. It is part of that person's job to be able to explain his request to you.

Citizens should ask politicians questions to make sure they are doing what is best for the community.

People in authority should always be able to explain their choices. In government, this is known as transparency. People, like politicians, who have been given authority have a greater responsibility to listen to their community. A good authority figure makes people feel comfortable speaking their minds. They welcome questions and are willing to explain their decisions. This helps build trust within communities.

Fast Fact

Authority can be taken away from people. If a person is not fulfilling his obligations, his authority can be taken away.

Respecting Authority at Home and School

There are authority figures everywhere we go. At home, your parents or guardians are the authority on you! They are the people who not only know you the best, but they want what's best for you. Of course, part of being an authority figure can mean enforcing rules that aren't fun. Your parents might ask you to do things you don't enjoy, like going to bed or eating your vegetables. They know that proper sleep and good nutrition are necessary to grow up healthy.

A babysitter is the authority figure when your parents go out.

Sometimes when your parents go out they will hire a babysitter. Your parents give babysitters the authority to enforce your family rules while they are away. It is also a babysitter's responsibility to keep you safe. When your babysitter asks you to do something, you should show her the same respect that you would show your parents.

Helps You Learn

Authority figures are helpful. In school, your teacher is the authority on your education. If you're having trouble in a topic, you can always ask your teacher help. Teachers assign homework that will help you remember your lessons. When your teacher assigns work, you should do your best to complete it. As teachers grade your homework, they can figure out which parts of the lesson you're having trouble with. When your teacher knows what you're having trouble with, she can help you focus on that area. Respecting your teacher's authority helps you be a better student.

Fast Fact

Teachers must earn a teaching certificate before working in schools.

Citizens Respect Authority

Citizens have a duty to respect authority. Many people in our community are authority figures on different things. During times of crisis, people with authority work together to ensure everyone in the community is safe. Meteorologists study the weather. During a hurricane, they are the authorities on the storm. They tell the people in the government what may happen and how to keep people safe during bad weather. When storms look very dangerous, local governments may order citizens to evacuate.

A meteorologist has special training that makes him an authority on dangerous weather.

Respecting Authority Keeps Us Safe

Not respecting authority can have negative consequences. When people do not respect the authority of the local politicians and meteorologists as a storm approaches, they may choose not to evacuate when they are told to. By not

evacuating, citizens put themselves in danger. They also endanger the first responders, who are responsible for rescuing people caught in the storm. When someone in authority tells you something is dangerous, you should listen! They are trying to keep you safe.

> **Fast Fact**
> Politicians hold town hall meetings where citizens can ask them questions.

Helping Authority Do What's Right

Good citizens know when to question authority. As citizens, we give politicians the authority to write laws and make decisions for the country. These laws affect everyone in the community. Good citizens are active in their

Good communication is an important part of being an authority figure.

government. They ask questions about new laws and make sure no other citizens will be hurt by them. By doing so, citizens can make sure that their representatives are making the right choices for everyone in the country. Good politicians ask other people with authority for advice when they are making decisions.

People with authority want to use their knowledge to make their communities better places. Knowing when to respect authority and when not to is an important part of being a good citizen.

ACTIVITY: WHO'S IN CHARGE?

There are people in authority everywhere we go. Whether we are at school, at home, or out in our community, there are people in charge. Think about the people in authority in your life.

- Make a poster to show examples of authority. Divide it into three parts: Home, School, and Community.

- In each section, include a picture of the people who are in authority there. You can draw the picture or find one on the internet.

- For example, in the Community section, think about people who keep us safe and people who are in charge. Police officers, doctors, and business owners are all people in authority.

- Include a short explanation of who each person is and why we should respect them.

LEARN MORE

Books

Boritzer, Etan. *What Is Respect?* Los Angeles, CA: Veronica Lane, 2016.

Coan, Sharon. *Being a Good Citizen.* Huntington Beach, CA: Teacher Created Material, 2015

Pegis, Jessica. *What Is Citizenship?* New York, NY: Crabtree, 2017

Websites

The Constitution for Kids
Usconstitution.net/constkidsK.html
Learn the history of the United States Constitution and Bill of Rights.

Stories About Respect
freestoriesforkids.com/tales-for-kids/values-and-virtues/stories-about-respect
Read and listen to children's stories about respect.

INDEX

Published in 2019 by Enslow Publishing, LLC.
101 W. 23rd Street, Suite 240, New York, NY 10011

Copyright © 2019 by Enslow Publishing, LLC.

All rights reserved.

No part of this book may be reproduced by any means without the written permission of the publisher.

Library of Congress Cataloging-in-Publication Data

Names: Santos, Rita, author.
Title: Zoom in on respect for authority / Rita Santos.
Description: New York, NY : Enslow Publishing, 2019. | Series: Zoom in on civic virtues | Audience: K-4 | Includes bibliographical references and index.
Identifiers: LCCN 2017048188| ISBN 9780766097797 (library bound) | ISBN 9780766097803 (pbk.) | ISBN 9780766097810 (6 pack)
Subjects: LCSH: Authority—Juvenile literature. | Respect—Juvenile literature. | Citizenship—Juvenile literature.
Classification: LCC HM1251 .S26 2019 | DDC 303.3/6—dc23
LC record available at https://lccn.loc.gov/2017048188

Printed in the United States of America

To Our Readers: We have done our best to make sure all website addresses in this book were active and appropriate when we went to press. However, the author and the publisher have no control over and assume no liability for the material available on those websites or on any websites they may link to. Any comments or suggestions can be sent by e-mail to customerservice@enslow.com.

Photo Credits: Cover, p. 1 John Roman Images/Shutterstock.com; p. 4 Andy Sacks/Photographer's Choice/Getty Images; p. 7 goodluz/Shutterstock.com; p. 10 Gregg Vignal/Alamy Stock Photo; pp. 12, 16 © iStockphoto.com/Steve Debenport; p. 15 BlueSkyImage/Shutterstock.com; p. 19 age fotostock/Alamy Stock Photo; p. 21 Blend Images/Shutterstock.com; p. 23 Rawpixel.com/Shutterstock.com; pp. 2, 3, 22 back cover ProStockStudio/Shutterstock.com; illustrated child with ball pp. 5, 9, 14, 1 MatoomMi/Shutterstock.com.